€4.00

HANGED FOR MURDER

IRISH STATE EXECUTIONS

Tim Carey wrote the bestselling *Mountjoy – The Story of a Prison* (2000), *Hanged for Ireland* (2001) and *Croke Park – A History* (2004), and he co-wrote *The Martello Towers of Dublin* (2012). A regular media contributor, he is a graduate of Trinity College and University College Dublin, and is currently heritage officer with Dún Laoghaire-Rathdown County Council.

Follow him on Twitter @tim_carey1

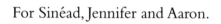
For Sinéad, Jennifer and Aaron.

HANGED FOR MURDER

IRISH STATE EXECUTIONS

TIM CAREY

The Collins Press

FIRST PUBLISHED IN 2013 BY
The Collins Press
West Link Park
Doughcloyne
Wilton
Cork

A catalogue record for this book is available from the British Library

Paperback ISBN: 9781848891869
PDF eBook ISBN: 9781848898172
EPUB eBook ISBN: 9781848898189
Kindle eBook ISBN: 9781848898196

Typesetting by David Prendergast
Typeset in Bembo 10.5/14.5pt
Printed in Malta by Gutenberg Press Limited

Contents

Acknowledgements

First and foremost, I would like to thank all of those who were involved with the four series of *Ceart agus Coir* that were broadcast by TG4 and which laid the foundations for this book. In particular, I would like to thank sincerely Mike Keane, director of Midas Productions and Reelgood Facilities, and Rosie Nic Cionnaith. I am also very grateful to Edel Quinn, Finnuala Ní Chíobháin, Catherine Quinn, Cleona Nic Chormaic, Cleona Ní Chrualaoí, Colm Bairéad and Cara Ronan.

I am indebted to Sean Reynolds of the Mountjoy Prison Museum whose insights into the prison's history were invaluable. I would also like to thank Jim Mitchell and Sean Aylaward, former director, of the Irish Prison Service for allowing access to prison files and for generally being extremely supportive of the various prison research projects I have undertaken.

A huge debt of gratitude is due to the staff of the National Archives of Ireland, in particular the former Director David Craig and Acting Director Frances Magee; Aideen Ireland, Head of Reader Services; archivist Gregory O'Connor; and last, but by no means least, the staff of the reading room, including Ken Robinson, Christy Allen, David O'Neill and Paddy Sarsfield, who dealt with my queries with great patience and were always helpful. Many thanks also to the National Library of Ireland and its reading room staff.

The advice and support of my agent, Sallyanne Sweeney of Watson, Little, was greatly appreciated. Thanks are also due to Vanessa O'Loughlin of www.writing.ie. My employers Dún Laoghaire-Rathdown County Council have always been supportive of my writing endeavours and for that I am very grateful.

The family of Sean Kavanagh, former Governor of Mountjoy Prison, very kindly made his papers available to me during various periods of research. Professor Ian O'Donnell, Head of the Institute of Criminology in University College Dublin, was most generous with his encouragement, support and advice. The late Marcus Burke gave valuable insights into the Harry Gleeson case; as did the members of the Justice for Harry Gleeson Group. Thanks are also due to Des Nix.

I am extremely grateful to my wife Sinéad and children Jennifer and Aaron for their support and encouragement throughout this project. Sinéad also assisted by reading the many drafts and making many helpful suggestions and comments. Both she and our children, put up with being without me for a prolonged period, so now I owe them …

Finally, I would like to thank Gillian Hennessy and all at The Collins Press for being excellent publishers.

Tim Carey

October 2013

Introduction

The Executions

Behind the walls of Mountjoy Prison on Dublin's North Circular Road lie the remains of twenty-eight men and one woman who, between 1923 and 1954, were convicted of 'common' murder and executed in the prison's hang house. This book tells their stories.

To most, the majority of people who feature in this book will be completely unknown. These are not people whose lives have been celebrated, whose deeds have been widely regaled. A few publications have previously cast light on some of these stories. Marcus Bourke's *Murder at Marlhill – Was Harry Gleeson Innocent?* and Dermot Walsh's *Beneath Cannock's Clock – The Last Man Hanged in Ireland* give detailed accounts of two of the execution cases. Kenneth Deale's *Beyond Any Reasonable Doubt?* (1971) looks at a variety of famous trials that include some of those which ended in an execution. Terry Prone's *Irish Murders* (Vols I and II, 1992 and 1994) also included some of the executed. However, none looked comprehensively at all of those who were put to death by the state.

Their trials took place at Green Street Courthouse, Dublin, and after the juries returned guilty verdicts, the presiding judges donned their black caps – not caps, as such, but small square pieces of black silk – and read out the death sentences:

> The sentence of the court are and it is ordered and adjudged that you [name of prisoner] be taken from the bar of the Court where you now stand to the prison from whence you last came and that on [day] the [date] day of [month] in the year of Our Lord [year written out] you be taken to the common place of execution in the prison in which you shall then be confined, and that you be then and there hanged by the neck until you be dead and that your body be buried within the walls of the prison in which the aforesaid Judgement of Death shall be executed upon you.

What happened next was clearly outlined in the prison's administrative documents. For each of the twenty-nine executions the process was the same.

From the moment a condemned prisoner was returned to Mountjoy two warders remained with them at all times, to ensure that they did not kill themselves and cheat the Irish state, on behalf of the people, of exacting its retribution. It was also their responsibility to help to keep the prisoner's spirits up, to make their last days pass as easily as possible. For their comfort the prisoner would be given cigarettes, an improved diet – though there was no request granted for a last meal – and other small luxuries, including newspapers and board games such as chess and draughts. The prisoner would then be put into the 'condemned cell', a large double cell located near the execution chamber at the end of D wing that allowed the prisoner to be brought to the hang house quickly when their time came.

Once the government had decided against a reprieve the governor would send word to the executioner, giving them the date of the hanging – they were always carried out at 8.00 a.m.

Though a new state had come into being and there was

some discussion about hiring an Irish executioner, for the sake of expediency and because of the perceived difficulty of getting an Irishman to take on a job that had so recently involved the execution of republican prisoners by the British, the Irish authorities came to an arrangement with Britain's executioners to continue to carry out the role. Apart from the first, who was executed by John Ellis, all of the twenty-nine executions in Mountjoy were carried out by members of the Pierrepoint family – most were carried out by Tom, with the last four by Albert. However, well into the period with which this book deals there was one short-lived attempt by de Valera's government to train an Irish hangman. His name was James O'Sullivan and he was from Cork but to protect his identity he operated under the false name 'Thomas Johnston'.

In a travel document issued by the authorities James O'Sullivan travelled to Strangeways Prison, Manchester, in 1945 to learn the skills needed to hang a person. However, Albert Pierrepoint was far from impressed. In his autobiography, *Executioner*, he described 'Johnston' as 'old and short and timid. When I first took him into the execution chamber his face went white as chalk.'

In 1947 James O'Sullivan was due to execute Joseph McManus. However, he told Sean Kavanagh, the prison governor, that he was not yet ready to conduct a hanging on his own. He asked that 'our friend' come over so that he could watch him do another execution.

Pierrepoint duly arrived the night before the execution with the arrangement apparently being that he would act as Johnston's assistant. However, when he set about preparing the hang house for the next morning he saw that his Irish colleague had forgotten all his training. The next morning, to the visible relief of 'Johnston', Governor Kavanagh asked Pierrepoint if he would carry out the execution. After McManus was hanged, James O'Sullivan left and was never seen in the prison again. The brief experiment of employing an Irish hangman was over.

When the executioner arrived at the prison the night before a hanging he was told the height and weight of the condemned prisoner and this allowed him to calculate the length of rope he would need to hang the person successfully. The aim was to achieve death swiftly by 'the dislocation of the neck' – usually the breaking of the third or fourth vertebra.

Estimating the proper length of rope was not an academic exercise: if the rope was too long the prisoner could be decapitated; too short and they would die a slow death by strangulation. A Table of Drops, first developed in the second half of the nineteenth century, assisted the executioner in his calculation. But the length could be adjusted depending on the prisoner's physique so the executioner would surreptitiously observe the prisoner, usually when they were brought out for exercise, and make any necessary adjustments to his calculation.

After he checked the prison scaffold to ensure that it was working properly, he readied the rope. The rope used at executions was not the 'hangman's noose' of films, but a rope with a metal eye at one end through which the other end would pass. A bag of sand the same weight as the prisoner, or 'culprit' as they were referred to in the original instructions, was tied to the rope and dropped the same length that the prisoner would be dropped the following day. The bag was left hanging overnight so as to take the 'stretch' out of the rope.

Up until their final night the prisoner would be permitted visits from family and perhaps a close friend. But on their last night their only companions were the chaplain and two of the warders who had been with them for just over three weeks (this was the usual length of time between the end of the trial and the execution). It was reported that they generally passed their last hours sleeping or playing cards or draughts with the warders. However, we have no idea what it must have been like for these twenty-nine people to know the very minute of their deaths and to feel the seconds pass by.

At around 7.15 a.m. the chaplain said Mass in the prisoner's cell. Then, shortly before 8 o'clock, the door would suddenly open and some of the most terrifying seconds imaginable would begin.

The prisoner's arms were quickly pinioned, or tied closely, to their body. Then the procession, comprised of the prisoner, the sheriff of the county where the crime had been committed, the priest, the governor, prison warders and the hangman, would quickly walk the short distance to the hang house. Once the prisoner was in position on the centre of the trapdoors their legs were strapped tightly, a white linen cap was placed over their head and the rope slipped around their neck. The rope's metal eye was positioned in front of the angle of the lower jaw so that when the prisoner started falling after the trapdoor opened it would move to under the chin and snap the head back, thus breaking the vertebrae. Warders stood on either side of the prisoner to hold him steady – they stood on wooden planks that spanned the trapdoors. Once the executioner was satisfied he pulled the lever that opened the trapdoors. Then all would be quiet.

The prisoner would be left hanging for an hour – a precaution taken in case they did not die instantly and had to be left to strangle to death.

The prison bell would toll and a brief note would be pinned to the prison gate announcing to whomever had waited outside the prison – family, friends, the curious or sympathetic – that the death sentence had been carried out.

Not surprisingly the newspaper accounts based on the words of prison staff invariably stated that the prisoner was calm, or perhaps showed some signs of nervousness, but that the execution went off as planned. In the reports, nobody screamed or cried.

An hour later the body would be taken down and brought to a temporary morgue where the doctor would ascertain the cause of death – in every case it was listed as the breaking of one or two of the vertebrae.

The governor would later fill out a form in which he rated the performance of the executioner. Did he carry out his duty well? Was his general demeanour and appearance satisfactory? Did he show suitable mental and physical capacity? Was there any reason to believe he would give an interview to the press? Was there anything to show, either before or after the execution, that he was not a suitable person?

At around midday, with all the paperwork completed, the prisoner would be buried in the grounds of the prison in the presence of the relevant chaplain and two prisoners acting as gravediggers.

The first five people convicted of murder who were executed in Mountjoy Prison after independence were buried in the grounds of what was then the female prison (it is now St Patrick's Institution). However, due to a Deputy Governor's objection that those burials had been near his living quarters, a new burial ground was chosen in the male prison. The yard selected was the one beside the Infirmary at the rear of the prison. The first to be buried there was Felix McMullen who was executed on 1 August 1924.

For a reason that is not known, and might just be put down to apathy on the part of the authorities, the locations of the graves of the twenty-nine were neither marked on the ground nor on a map. The practice in England had been to carve the convict number of the prisoner in a wall near their burial site: when the British left the prison they left a map showing the graves of the ten republicans executed during the War of Independence – as it turned out the map proved to be perfectly accurate when, eight decades later, those bodies were disinterred and given state funerals in Glasnevin. However, no such map exists in the prison files and searches of the Mountjoy's walls have revealed no marks. To this day no one knows the exact burial place of almost all of the twenty-nine (the resting place of two are believed to be known from information given by prison staff some years ago).

This unnecessary indignity inflicted on the executed and their memory might well have future implications. If the Mountjoy Prison site is ever sold and redeveloped the thorny issue of finding and identifying the twenty-nine bodies (in addition to others buried in the prison grounds) will have to be addressed. Equally, in the event that a relative of one of the executed successfully challenges the sentence under which they were executed they might well make the obvious request to have the body of their relative disinterred from the grounds for proper burial elsewhere. The difficulty then will be that no one will know which one is their relative. In the end, the only way of adequately resolving the issue, should such an occasion arise and should all the families of the twenty-nine agree, would be a full scale archaeological excavation and DNA testing.

The Legal Process
There are a number of aspects of the cases that are common to most and that are best addressed here rather than within the body of each chapter.

A brief word on the type of evidence on which the twenty-nine were convicted is needed because the vast majority were convicted on 'circumstantial evidence'. To those, like the author, without a legal background, the importance of circumstantial evidence is often misunderstood. Almost by its nature the crime of murder is a secret one, carried out by people away from potential witnesses. Therefore, prosecution lawyers resorted to circumstantial evidence in most trials. As the judges explained to the juries it was not something they should have felt uncomfortable about. One should also bear in mind that this was a time when forensic evidence was primitive and DNA evidence non-existent.

Given today's legal time frames it was a remarkably swift process from arrest to execution. In only one of the cases was it more than a year, with the shortest being just under three months. The average time between arrest and execution was somewhere between four and five months. Trials were short, sometime peremptorily so. The briefest trial lasted just half a day, the longest seventeen. The least amount of time a jury spent considering a case was a mere ten minutes, the most just over four hours. The execution date for a prisoner was set for just over three weeks after the end of the trial. However, that date would be changed if an appeal was lodged against the conviction.

The Court of Criminal Appeal was established in 1924 and was the first recourse for a legal team following a conviction. It is sometimes easy to look back on the newspaper reports and court transcripts and think that a different decision might have been reached. However, the Court of Criminal Appeal was careful about overturning any decision reached by a jury. While they were given a transcript of the trial and could carefully study each word, they were aware that what they missed out on was the vital information that the jury would have had access to, namely, how convincing or otherwise a witness had been when they took the stand. To appreciate the distinction, think of the difference between reading the words of a politician and hearing them spoken first-hand. However, the Court of Appeal was also inherently conservative. Made up of two High Court judges, who were the same rank as the trial judge, and a Supreme Court judge, the court seemed to have been loath to overturn one of the decisions. Of the twenty-nine cases in this publication, just one – Lehman – had a conviction overturned by the Court of Appeal; he was subsequently convicted at a second trial. When reading some of these cases one could reasonably think that the number should have been somewhat higher.

The last chance for a convicted prisoner was for the government to decide to reprieve them. Any recommendation to mercy by a jury was forwarded to the government, while reports were often requested from various quarters including the Mountjoy medical officer and chaplain as well as the gardaí who had investigated the case. In some cases, petitions for a reprieve – sometimes with up to 7,000 signatures – were also sent to the government, while occasionally personal contacts the defendants or their supporters might have had provided a direct line to a government figure.

One should bear in mind that during the period 1923–1954 when the twenty-nine were executed, over forty condemned prisoners were reprieved. These men and women were then sentenced to penal servitude for life but, in general, were released after fewer than ten years and, in at least nine cases, within less than three years. There was a fine line between being buried in the prison grounds and serving a relatively short time in prison.

One must also be careful to remember that with the passage of time there can be a tendency to look on crimes – committed over sixty years ago – in a different way than we would view the same crimes today. There is a natural inclination to be less punitively minded towards people who no longer present a threat to us. However, after reading the cases there are some voices in the burial grounds of Mountjoy that are more insistent than others. These are the ones that whisper, 'Are you sure I did it? Are you sure it was me?'

Of the twenty-nine cases there are at least four that stand out as ones where the wrong decision may have been reached: Daniel Doherty's insanity defence seemed to have been very strong; there appeared to be no safe evidence on which David O'Shea was convicted; almost all the evidence against Joseph McManus could equally have been applied to another man; and Harry Gleeson has been thought innocent by many people ever since his conviction in 1941 and may well be the greatest miscarriage of justice in the history of the Irish State.

The Harry Gleeson file has been one of the most requested capital case files in the National Archives since the mid-1990s. In fact, the Gleeson file now has a special number and table in the Four Courts store because it has been called up so often. Of all the cases this is the one that is probably most likely to yield a change in verdict. However, it is understood that when Marcus Bourke's book, *Murder at Marlhill – Was Harry Gleeson Innocent?*, was published the file was recalled by the Department of Justice and reviewed. No action was taken following this review.

The people who continue to believe that Harry Gleeson and others of those executed (including the family of James Myles, executed in 1926) were innocent face the difficulty that all of the people who might have been involved in the case and who could provide new evidence are now, in all likelihood, dead.

Two aspects of the legal system under which these twenty-nine people were tried deserve mention. One is what can only be described as a reprehensible policy that existed in Ireland until 1937. It was that for those who could not afford their own defence counsel, and these were nearly all of the defendants, a junior counsel acted on their behalf. That this was done at trials where people's lives were at stake can only be described as disgraceful. At the trials their solitary junior counsels, with little administrative back up, were up against one or two, and in some cases even three, senior counsels and all the administrative and other support they came with. This skewed the scales of justice considerably against the defendants. How this affected the outcomes of any of the trials is not clear, but it most certainly must have had some effect.

The second issue was the role that the judges played at the trials. Their main purpose was to ensure that a trial was conducted correctly under the law and in a fair manner. However, they often influenced trials to a very marked degree. They would correctly point out to the jury that on rules of law the jury needed to follow the judge's advice, but on deciding whether evidence presented to them was a 'fact' or not they said that was for the jury to decide.

However, that did not stop judges from expressing their opinions on the 'facts', sometimes to a telling extent. How a judge treated a witness during their questioning could also have had a significant, though perhaps unquantifiable, influence on the outcome. At a time when authority figures enjoyed a revered status and were almost beyond questioning, the influence of a judge at a trial could be very great indeed.

Some judges were hardly able to stop themselves from making comments during trials. Rarely did those comments favour the defendant. Some cases are borderline, others less so. While it might be unfair to describe any as hanging judges there are cases, particularly the David O'Shea case before Judge Hanna and the Harry Gleeson case before Judge Martin Maguire, in which it is hard not to believe that the judges played a central role in sending the men to their deaths. As this was also a time when there was almost universal and unquestioning acceptance of garda evidence, no matter how dubious, the scales of justice could not always be said to have been perfectly balanced.

The Executed

The aim of each chapter in this publication is to outline the main points of the case and answer the very basic question of why was that person convicted? What is their story? It is important to note that each case has been approached from the common sense viewpoint of a 'lay person'. It is fully admitted that another person reading the same material may highlight other issues or come to different conclusions.

The salient features of the stories associated with each case have been selected from trawling through witness depositions, trial transcripts, garda reports, medical reports and newspaper articles. This book necessarily concentrates its attention on the people who were executed and not on those whom they were convicted of killing. It is merely the nature of the subject matter and is not intended to glorify the person convicted of murder, or to garner sympathy towards them and the plight they endured in Mountjoy's execution chamber.

Unfortunately, there is an initial limitation to studying the cases of the executed because, due to a lack of detailed information relating to the first four of the executed (all of whom were hanged in the last two months of 1923), it is difficult to be certain about the specifics of the crimes for which they were convicted. Therefore, in this brief analysis of the capital punishment cases, they will be omitted and reference will be made only to the remaining twenty-five.

The twenty-five cases are all remarkably different. Each person lived in, and was convicted of committing their crimes, in certain specific circumstances. That there is unevenness to the treatment of the cases is simply a consequence of the nature of the stories and the amount and quality of information that is available in the various official files and news reports. A few are little more than detailed pen pictures of who they were and why they ended up in prison. Others are much more comprehensive with detailed background stories being outlined and legal issues discussed.

In 1946 English writer George Orwell wrote an article on the 'Decline of the English Murder' in which he lamented, from the voyeuristic point of view of the Sunday newspaper reader, the fact that murders were simply not what they used to be. He wistfully noted that there had been a marked decline in ones carried out under the sway of powerful emotions, where the victim and killer had a close relationship and, very often, shared last names. The modern trend that he noted was towards the more mundane and distant type of killing that lacked a background story of simmering resentment, loathing, lust and hatred. Thinking of the lack of interest people have in the now common 'gangland' murders, how we turn a newspaper page with indifference at a headline announcing another murder carried out with the dispassion of the contract killer, one can understand Orwell's argument. However, nearly all of the twenty-five had a 'background' story that, if not justifying the murders for which they were convicted, at least gave a context to them.

The first thing that one notices about these twenty-five cases is that all but three (McMullen, O'Neill and Manning) knew their victims. Nine were convicted of killing people who were related to them: three killed their wives (William O'Shea, Fleming and Lehman); three their brothers (O'Leary, McDermott and Kirwan); one their husband (Walsh); one their uncle (Talbot); and one their cousin (Doherty). Two (Smyth and Gambon) had killed people whom they described as their closest friends. Three (McCabe, Toal and Cox) killed people they either worked with or were employed by. Six (Gaffney, Fleming, Gleeson, McManus, Doherty and McHugh) had been involved, or allegedly been involved, in what would have been described as 'immoral relationships' that had some bearing on the reason for the murder. But perhaps the most remarkable statistic to come out of this analysis is that ten of the twenty-four men who were executed had recently become, or were about to become, fathers. Six had partners or wives who had recently given birth (McCabe, Hornick, Smyth, William O'Shea, Lehman and McManus) while three (Fleming, Gambon and Manning) had wives who gave birth to children after their father's arrest or execution. One pregnant woman was killed in a murder (Doherty).

Nine of the twenty-five had been convicted of a crime prior to committing the ultimate crime of all, murder. These were Talbot, McCabe, Toal, Cox, Kelly, Kirwan, Lehman, McManus and Gambon. However, of these, only Kirwan, McCabe and Lehman had previously been convicted of a serious crime; the others had committed petty offences. Therefore, the majority were people whose first crime was murder. Three had been in industrial schools (Toal, Kelly and Gambon). Six had military backgrounds and had been in the British, American or Irish armies or the Irish Republican Army (IRA)

(Gaffney, McMullen, Myles, Cox, Lehman and McManus). Though alcohol is present in most of the stories, surprisingly in just five cases was it believed to have been a contributing factor to the murder. Perhaps a sign that the land issue had well and truly been settled was that just three cases – those of O'Leary, McDermott and Kirwan – could have been said to have involved land.

An interesting aspect of the murders relating to the twenty-five cases is that the vast majority took place outside of the major urban areas. In fact, just six of the twenty-five could be called 'city crimes' with two taking place in Limerick (Cox and Manning) and four in Dublin (McCabe, Fleming, Lehman and Gambon). Of the rest, three could be described as taking place in towns, or their immediate hinterlands (McMullen in Baltinglass, County Wicklow; McHugh in New Ross, County Wexford; and McManus in Navan, County Meath). The remainder took place in 'rural' areas of counties Kerry (Gaffney), Cork (O'Leary and David O'Shea), Louth (Myles), Wicklow (O'Neill), Roscommon (McDermott), Wexford (Hornick), Laois (Smyth), Donegal (Doherty), Sligo (Kelly), Tipperary (Gleeson), Offaly (Kirwan) and Waterford (William O'Shea). Drawing any conclusion from this distribution without analysing all the capital cases during the time period is not possible. The fact that the cases were tried in the city of Dublin in front of a jury made up generally of middle- and upper-class Dublin residents may have been a contributory factor in the geographic spread of the convictions. These Dublin juries may have been quicker to convict those from rural areas – some of which were very remote from the urban Dublin and its social mores – than they were to convict those from the capital and other urban areas.

At least nine of the twenty-five cases (Gaffney, Talbot, Walsh, McHugh, Fleming, Doherty, Gleeson, Lehman and McManus) involved 'immoral' or alleged 'immoral' relationships. This seems a very high number accounting as they do for nearly one-third of the total number of cases. Whether this represents a higher percentage than in the total capital cases is not known. But the question arises as to whether juries were more prone to convict someone when there was evidence of an 'immoral relationship'? Equally, were governments less likely to reprieve them?

Four (David O'Shea, O'Neill, Kelly and Manning) committed murders that were either sexually motivated or were accompanied by sexual violence.

The twenty-nine (including the first four) executions took place over the three decades that was a period of great change in Ireland. These decades were the first three of the new state. Initially it was thought that capital punishment would not be part of the constitutional make-up of the new state as a reaction of associating the death penalty with British rule. However, the outbreak of the Civil War meant that it was included in the laws of the new state. But it should be noted that the last execution by the British, apart from the political executions of 1916 and the 1919–1921 era, had been in 1911 and in the last twenty-one years of British rule just twelve people were executed for common murder.

It is likely that if the political situation had been different capital punishment for criminals would have been abolished. However, it was kept on for political reasons and, though the ending of the Civil War removed the immediate reason for its retention, successive governments could not bring themselves to remove it. Therefore, with it on the books the courts were forced to revert to it in murder cases. The irony of this situation is that when the state did execute IRA members, they did not use the existing law under which common criminals were executed but resorted to military tribunals under emergency legislation. The retention of capital punishment for 'common murder', which resulted in twenty-nine executions, was something of an unnecessary accident. A recent summary of the executions for murder, as well as political offences, was given in

David M. Doyle and Ian O'Donnell's 'The Death Penalty in Post-Independence Ireland' in the *Journal of Legal History* 33 (1): 65–91).

The rate of executions varies considerably during the thirty-one years. The first was by far the most active decade in terms of executions with seventeen of the twenty-nine taking place between 1923 and 1933. This high rate can be partially explained by two main factors. The first was a violent feeling engendered by the brutality of the First World War, the War of Independence and Civil War, which created an atmosphere in which life was cheapened and death by violence, however inflicted, was more acceptable. The second factor was that, in the initial years of this period at least, there was lawlessness in parts of the country that the authorities were keen to clamp down on and exert a controlling influence.

The next decade, 1934–1943, saw eight people executed. The marked decline resulted from a distancing from the more violent era of 1914–1923 and a society settling down after significant upheavals. It was also a result of the declining homicide rate in Ireland – down from 5.7 per million of population in the late 1920s to 4.1 per million in the 1930s.

The final decade of capital punishment was by far the quietest. Between 1944 and 1954 the numbers executed fell to just four. Again this was the result of the decline in the homicide rate that, by the 1950s, had fallen to an historic low and was less than half the rate of the late 1920s. In addition, there was an increased aversion to the imposition of the death penalty with an increasing percentage of people convicted of murder being reprieved by the government. The last execution to take place in Ireland, and the last chapter in this book, was that of Michael Manning who was hanged in April 1954 and became the last person to be buried in an unmarked grave within the grounds of Mountjoy Prison.

1 William Downes, Dublin

Executed on 29 November 1923 for the murder of Captain Thomas Fitzgerald

Twenty-four-year-old William Downes was a dispatch rider in the new National Army and was stationed in Portobello Barracks, Dublin. On 19 October 1923, William, dressed in civilian clothes, and two other men, George Cullen and John McDonald (also dispatch riders) went to Rathborne's candle factory at Ashtown, north county Dublin. When they were there two of the men, one of whom was later identified as William Downes who had a revolver drawn, took £43. The three then fled on stolen bicycles. For a time, they were pursued by two of the factory staff who were also on bicycles. The alarm was raised and a car from the Criminal Investigation Division (CID) at Oriel House was sent to the area.

When the officers reached Dunsink they saw three men cycling fast down a hill. They overtook the cyclists, stopped the car and pursued them. William was captured but his accomplices fled. One detective, Captain Thomas Fitzgerald, stayed with William at the car while the other three chased the remaining raiders. A short time later, the three detectives returned empty-handed to the car only to find that William Downes was missing and Fitzgerald had been shot. The detective died just minutes later.

That evening William was captured at Leitrim Place in Dublin in possession of a revolver that had been recently fired.

According to a statement William gave police, Captain Fitzgerald had ordered him to sit in the car beside him. When the detective started to reverse the car William shot Fitzgerald and left the scene.

William's trial took place just eleven days after his arrest and lasted for a day. When the jury retired to consider the verdict it took them just twenty minutes to find him guilty. When Downes was asked if he had anything to say, he told the court that he had been forced to sign the statement – a gun had been held to his head by members of the CID. He said that the reason he had shot Fitzgerald was that the detective was going to shoot him and he had fired in self-defence. He concluded, 'I swear that by almighty God.'

One month later, on 29 November 1923, William Downes was executed for the murder of Thomas Fitzgerald. He was the first non-political person to be executed by the new Irish State and the first to be executed in Ireland since 1911.

2 Thomas Delaney, Offaly

Executed on 12 December 1923 for the murder of Patrick Horan

Thomas Delaney was found guilty of the murder of seventy-four-year-old Patrick Horan in Banagher, County Offaly. Thomas, a twenty-eight-year-old labourer, was an ex-Irish guardsman who had been badly injured in the jaw and neck during the Great War. After being out of action for nine months he returned but was soon caught in a gas attack in France. Patrick Horan was a well-off shopkeeper who lived alone. Early in the morning of 27 June 1923 neighbours heard the cry of 'murder' from Patrick Horan's house. When two neighbours went in they found Patrick bleeding badly. Once in the hall they saw Thomas Delaney with blood on his hands and clothes. He was holding part of a broken pair of tongs. When one of the neighbours took hold of Thomas he told him, 'I am mad.' A few days later, Patrick Horan died of his injuries.

After the attack on Patrick, Thomas told the guards, 'On the morning of June 27, I went into Mr Horan's house. When he saw me he rushed at me, and then I got so excited I did not know what happened after.' At the end of his trial, the jury took just three minutes to find him guilty. Asked if he had anything to say he replied, 'I have nothing to say my Lord.' Delaney was executed on 12 December 1923.

3 Thomas McDonagh, Roscommon

Executed on 12 December 1923 for the murder of Ellen Rogers

In 1922, forty-eight-year-old Thomas McDonagh lived next door to thirty-four-year-old Ellen Rogers in Loughglynn, County Roscommon. The two had previously had a falling out over a broken window. On 24 May, a few months after the new Irish State was formed, Thomas asked her to go as security for him on a loan of £130. She refused. The next morning Thomas went into her house and shot her dead. He then gave himself up to an IRA policeman.

Thomas was kept in custody until the end of the Civil War. His trial finally took place on 16 November 1923 – it was on the same day as Thomas Delaney's. Thomas McDonagh pleaded insanity but after forty minutes the jury found him guilty. It was the only time in the history of capital punishment in Ireland that two people were tried and convicted of two different murders on the same day. Thomas McDonagh was hanged on the same day as Thomas Delaney, 12 December 1923.

4 Peter Hynes, Meath

Executed on 15 December 1923 for the murder of Thomas
Grimstone

On 14 January 1922 Thomas Grimstone, a former soldier –
known as 'Tommy the Soldier' – who was believed to have
been living in Cootehill, County Cavan, was outside Drogheda,
on Plattin Road on the Meath side of the county border. He was
looking for a bed for the night, rather than the prospect of sleeping
out in the open when he met Peter Hynes, a former barber and
general labourer.

Peter, who had been drinking, asked Tommy if he was a soldier.
When Tommy replied that he was, Peter asked if he was an Irishman.
When he said he was, Peter told him, 'Come along with me and I
won't see you out.' Tommy's luck seemed to have been in. However,
during the night Peter beat Tommy to death with an iron bar.

Peter later said that the reason he had killed Tommy was that
during the night he saw him reach for something. He thought he
was getting a revolver. After he killed Tommy – whose face was
beaten beyond recognition – Peter put his body under his bed and
slept over him for the night. The next day he told a friend, 'I found
a "Tan" in my bed last night and knocked his brains out.' After he
dumped his body nearby it was discovered by members of the IRA
and Peter was arrested.

Having spent nearly two years in prison Peter was finally tried for murder. After an absence of fifteen minutes the jury returned the guilty verdict. When Hynes was sentenced he replied, 'All I have got to say is, it is time the job was finished.' He was executed on 15 December 1923.

5 Jeremiah Gaffney, Kerry

Executed on 13 March 1924 for the murder of Tom Brosnan

Bad Times Return to Kerry

The official hostilities of the Irish Civil War may have ended in April 1923 with a general election held in August, but the process of 'normalising' even the most basic aspects of Irish society was going to take some time. In December 1923 the Free State was only starting to come to grips with one of the most basic issues facing any society, that of law and order. In November and December the executions of four 'common murderers' in quick succession had been part of this process. However, just as these were taking place, what appeared to be one of the last struggles of the Civil War was being played out in Scartaglin, County Kerry.

On 3 December, Sergeant Woods of the Scartaglin Civic Guards was killed by a group of 'Irregular' anti-Treaty forces. In response, the government sent twenty-five soldiers, under the command of a Lieutenant Gaffney, to the nearby town of Castleisland with the mission of pacifying the area and capturing those involved. According to his superior officer, Gaffney was to treat the area as his 'independent republic' – Gaffney was to deal with the situation as he saw fit.

Lieutenant Gaffney was twenty-four years old and unmarried. Originally from the Amiens Street area of Dublin he had served in the Dublin Guards before joining the National Army in early 1923. The lieutenant was familiar with the area, having been stationed in Scartaglin from May to August. It appeared that the killing of Sergeant Woods and the stationing of Gaffney and his troops had brought the old times back to this part of Kerry.

At 4 o'clock on the morning of 6 December Gaffney roused his men and headed to the village of Scartaglin, about 5 miles away. The soldiers proceeded to make their presence felt by patrolling the town and visiting a number of pubs. At 2.00 p.m., after having half a dozen or so drinks, they returned to Castleisland where the lieutenant continued drinking.

At 4.00 p.m. Gaffney ordered five soldiers – Sergeant O'Shea and Volunteers Leen, McNeill, Brosnan and O'Shea – to put on civilian clothes and get into a lorry driven by another solider, Vol. McCusker. Gaffney had one of the then fashionable 'Peter the Painter' Mauser revolvers strapped to his leg while the five soldiers carried rifles.

They drove the lorry, without lights, through the dark and stormy night and stopped at what was known as Danny Roche's crossroads, about a mile from Scartaglin. Before they started their operation Gaffney gathered his men around him and told them that if any of them ever opened their mouths about what was going to happen he would have them shot. Gaffney told Vol. McNeill, who was staying with the driver in the lorry, not to be alarmed if he heard any gunfire.

After the group of soldiers walked a short distance Gaffney swapped guns with Leen and told him to 'crease' Tom Brosnan. When he pointed to a house, Vol. Leen, Sergeant O'Shea and Vol. Brosnan (no known relation to Tom Brosnan) walked up to it and opened the front door.

The Brosnans

Cornelius and Johanna Brosnan lived with their eighteen-year-old son Tom. Johanna ran a small grocery and licensed business at the front of their house while Cornelius was a blacksmith with Tom working with him at his forge.

At the end of their day's work on 6 December Cornelius and Tom had returned home. Sometime between 6 and 6.30 p.m., after the family had dinner, Tom, as was his usual evening routine, went to his grandmother's pub in the village. Had the evening been a normal one he would have returned sometime after 9.30 p.m.

After Tom left, Cornelius and Johanna remained chatting in the kitchen. Then they heard the front door open.

Cornelius went out and saw three men dressed in trench coats. From the dim light cast by a candle on a barrel he saw that at least two were armed – the man at the counter had a Peter the Painter and the one just inside the door had a rifle.

Cornelius did not recognise them but thought they must have been members of the National Army he had seen around the village earlier in the day. He said afterwards that he had not been overly concerned or frightened by the encounter. During the recent conflicts he had become well used to the military calling to the house. Inconveniences such as these had become a fact of life.

Leen, the only soldier to talk during the entire incident, asked for Tom. When Cornelius told him where his son had gone the soldier told him to bring them there.

When they got to the pub in Scartaglin, Cornelius called Tom out from the back kitchen – a Civic Guard was there but he too thought the situation quite normal. The three soldiers and father and son walked back to Brosnans' with Leen walking with Tom and chatting about the weather. There seemed to be no portent about what was to come. When they got back to the house, Leen – perhaps to steel himself for what he was about to do – asked for some whiskey. They had none but Cornelius said that Tom could go for some. Leen told him it didn't matter. Anyway, he wanted Tom to go up the road with him.

As the soldiers left with Tom, Cornelius tried to follow but Leen turned and told him, 'You can remain there; he will be back in a few minutes.' As the minutes ticked by he became increasingly anxious about his son. 'I got uneasy,' he later said, 'and I went to the chapel cross and was there for five or ten minutes listening to hear any sound. I went to John Kerin's house. I went to my mother's house and then back to my own house.'

In the meantime Leen, followed by Sergeant O'Shea and Vol. Brosnan, walked Tom down the road where they met Lieutenant Gaffney and Vol. O'Shea. While the others stopped, Leen and Tom walked on. Shortly afterwards six shots from a Peter the Painter were heard above the howl of the wind.

When Vol. Brosnan and Sergeant O'Shea walked back to the lorry they passed Tom's body lying on the road 'without a stir in him'. However, Tom was just pretending to be dead at that stage because, though Leen had fired six shots, Tom had been hit just once in the leg – it was likely that Leen had intentionally missed with the five other shots. Soon the soldiers caught up with Leen but as they made their way back to the truck they heard two rifle shots from behind. Then Lieutenant Gaffney caught up with them and told Leen, 'You did not shoot him right at all; I had to put two more shots through him myself.'

As they drove back to Castleisland Gaffney warned his men, 'Don't speak about the "creasing" of that fellow, boys.'

Meanwhile, as the military lorry made its way back to Castleisland Cornelius found his son's lifeless body, face down on the road a short distance from the village and only a few hundred yards from his home. He had been shot three times, twice in the back of the thigh and once in the lower part of the back. It was later ascertained from the oblique angle that one of the bullets had travelled through the body that it had been fired into his back while he had been lying face down on the ground.

The Aftermath of the Killing

Initial press reports suggested that Tom Brosnan, like Sergeant Woods a few days earlier, had been killed by 'Irregulars'. However, the Kerry brigade of the IRA took the somewhat unusual step of writing a letter to the *Cork Examiner* in which they stated: 'We emphatically repudiate the insinuation, and we can confidently assure the public that the arms used in this raid and murder do not belong to the IRA in this country and that no Republican soldier was implicated in the crime … We earnestly hope that the raiders, murderers and would-be murderers will be brought to justice quickly.' The subsequent inquest into Tom's death sensationally concluded that he had not died at the hands of the anti-Treaty IRA but had died from 'bullet wounds inflicted by members of the National Army'. The bad times seemed to have returned to that part of Kerry.

Apart from the outrage caused by the callous murder of a young man the killing was also an undoubted source of embarrassment to a government that was still trying to establish its legitimacy among some sections of the population. To convey its concern General Eoin O'Duffy, Head of the Civic Guards, was instructed to travel to Scartaglin. He was reported to have been visibly moved when he expressed his sympathy for their 'awful bereavement'.

A week after the killing of the eighteen-year-old, the National Army completed an internal inquiry that led to the detention of Lieutenant Gaffney and the six soldiers who had gone to Scartaglin that night. However, Leen almost immediately deserted from the army and when the remaining soldiers were transferred to Tralee Gaffney escaped – his escape led to a row between the civic guards and the military, with one report stating that the 'whole story is one of amateurs and reflects badly on our administration'.

A huge manhunt was started for Leen and Gaffney. After extensive searches Leen was captured in Liverpool and brought back to Dublin on 3 January 1924. Four days later he was charged with the murder of Tom Brosnan. On 9 January Gaffney's parents went to the police in Dublin Castle and told them that their son would give himself up that night. However, not wanting to take any chances the police scoured the city and found Gaffney at North Richmond Cottages on the north side of Dublin City, near where he used to live. Although armed with a Smith & Wesson revolver Gaffney offered no resistance.

The next day Gaffney was transferred to Tralee and was met by angry crowds – at one point Cornelius Brosnan came out from the crowd and tried to punch the prisoner. The lieutenant was then charged with feloniously, wilfully and with malice aforethought killing and murdering Thomas Brosnan.

The Trial

Jeremiah Gaffney's trial started on 13 February 1924 at the newly established Central Criminal Court in Dublin. He pleaded not guilty.

The prosecution described the crime as particularly atrocious: 'Under circumstances of the most deliberate, cold-blooded, and premeditated villainy at the insistence of a man who held the rank of lieutenant in the National Army, the youth was foully butchered in a manner so treacherous, so revolting that it would disgrace a tribe of savages.'

Gaffney had not made a statement to police and gave no evidence at his trial. However, detailed evidence against Gaffney was given by the soldiers who had been under his command that gave a clear picture of what had happened in Scartaglin on 6 December.

According to their testimony, Gaffney was their superior officer. It was under his orders that Tom Brosnan had been taken from his house and shot. Lieutenant Gaffney had also fired the fatal shots.

At the trial the alleged motive for the cold-blooded killing of Tom Brosnan centred not on any issue directly related to the Civil War but rather on Gaffney's relationship with a woman, Ellen Kane.

Ellen Kane was a maternity nurse who had been married to John Brosnan, a relation of Cornelius and Tom's. They had married four years earlier but separated shortly after the wedding because John's father had not approved of the marriage – the reason for this was not given in court. Some months later John left for America while Nurse Kane stayed in Scartaglin.

When Lieutenant Gaffney was stationed in the village during the summer of 1923 he and Nurse Kane started a relationship. Ellen moved into the house where Gaffney was billeted and even became known to some as 'Mrs Gaffney'. Though her husband had left her to go to America, the Brosnan family still thought she should have behaved as though she were married. According to Cornelius Brosnan all of the family objected to the relationship and there was on-going bad feeling between Ellen Kane and the Brosnans. When the military post in Scartaglin was broken up she went to Dublin for a time, presumably to be with Gaffney, but had since returned.

One of the soldiers alleged that Gaffney told him that the morning they had patrolled Scartaglin he had called to Ellen Kane's house. Ellen allegedly told Gaffney that Tom Brosnan had been involved in the killing of Sergeant Woods. It is not known if, in fact, she did say this because Ellen was not called as a witness at Gaffney's trial. It is possible that Gaffney had made it up to justify the killing to one of his soldiers. It is also possible that the killing of Tom Brosnan had been part of a personal vendetta Gaffney had held against the Brosnan family, one he hoped he would get away with in the disturbed conditions following the killing of Sergeant Woods. Whatever the truth might have been about the motive, Tom's father said that his son and Sergeant Woods had been 'the best of friends'.

After the prosecution had finished its case the defence counsel argued that the only evidence against Gaffney was given by accomplices who were trying to save themselves. It was also argued that Gaffney had not compelled Leen to shoot Tom Brosnan. The lieutenant's counsel also produced medical evidence relating to a serious accident he had suffered in 1915 that fractured his skull and resulted in a bone fragment the size of a coin being removed. The doctor who carried out the operation thought it would have left Gaffney incapable of dealing with problems that came up suddenly, if he was in an excited state. The defence also argued that the amount of drink taken on the day had seriously affected Gaffney's mind.

At 7.30 p.m. at the end of the second day of the trial, the judge finished his summing-up and the jury retired to consider their verdict. After fifty minutes, they returned to the courtroom and told the judge they were unable to reach a verdict. The judge was clearly not impressed and told them, 'We have been trying this case for two days. And I won't take a disagreement.' The foreman replied, 'I am afraid that there is no possible hope,' but the judge insisted they continue their deliberations.

At 10.30 p.m. the judge instructed that a message be sent to the jury asking if they were ready. Almost immediately the jury returned and announced that Jeremiah Gaffney had been found guilty of murder, with a recommendation to mercy. The judge set the date for Gaffney's execution as 13 March 1924.

Other Soldiers and Execution

Initially, all the soldiers who had been to Scartaglin on the night of 6 December 1923 had been put forward for trial. Vol. O'Shea had been tried with Gaffney but was acquitted as no evidence was brought against him. Charges of complicity in the murder were brought against Vols. McNeill, Brosnan and the lorry driver but these were dropped. However, the week after Gaffney's trial Vol. Leen and Sergeant O'Shea were tried for murder. Sergeant O'Shea was acquitted but Leen, who had admitted to shooting Tom Brosnan at least once, was found guilty and sentenced to death. His execution was scheduled for the week after Gaffney's.

Jeremiah Gaffney was executed in Mountjoy Prison as scheduled. But before he walked from the condemned cell to the hang house he wrote out a full confession in which he admitted complete responsibility for the murder of Tom Brosnan. He wrote that he had threatened to shoot Vol. Leen if he disobeyed his order and that Leen had only injured Brosnan but he – Gaffney – had shot Tom twice while he was trying to escape over a low fence. He asked that the confession be forwarded to the Minister for Home Affairs, Kevin O'Higgins.

As a result of Gaffney's confession, Leen's death sentence was commuted to penal servitude for life. After serving two years and three months in prison. Denis Leen was released on 8 May 1926.

6 Felix McMullen, Wicklow

Executed on 1 August 1924 for the murder of Sergeant Patrick
O'Halloran

The Bank Raid

On 28 January 1924 taxi driver James Smith of the LSE Motor
Company was dispatched to the Ormonde Hotel, on the
north side of the Dublin quays, where he picked up two men. Both
of them wore trench coats and light grey caps. One carried an
attaché case. They told Smith to drive them to Baltinglass, a village
over 35 miles away, in County Wicklow.

Felix McMullen, who Smith would later describe as the taller of
the two, was born in Derrylin, County Fermanagh, and was living
at 34 South William Street, Dublin. He was twenty-nine years old,
around 5 feet 10 inches tall with dark hair, dark complexion, thin
lips, square chin and dark eyebrows. He had an athletic build but
walked with a slight limp. McMullen had served in the British Army
for three years and fought in France during the Great War. After
the Provisional Government was established he enlisted in the new
National Army and became a Captain of the Special Infantry Corps.
After the end of the Civil War he was demobilised on 11 December
1923.

Peter Jordan, the shorter of the two, was from Adamstown,
County Wexford, and was living at 29 Paul Street, Dublin. He was

twenty-six years old and around 5 feet 6 inches tall with a fair complexion, round face, square jaw and heavy build. He had studied to be a national schoolteacher and fought with the IRA during the War of Independence. When the new state was founded he, like Felix, became a Captain of the Special Infantry Corps and, also like his accomplice, was demobilised on 11 December 1923.

These two men, until recently members of the forces of law and order, were about to become agents of disorder because, when they got into the taxi, they were on their way to hold up a bank.

Early 1924 was a time of great transition in Ireland. The Free State was trying to establish itself fully in the aftermath of a War of Independence and a Civil War and society was still in a state of flux. Felix and Peter were symptomatic of just one of the many problems that the new state faced – some of the recently demobilised soldiers were turning to lives of crime.

As the taxi approached the village of Baltinglass, nestled in the foothills of the Wicklow Mountains, Peter told the driver to stop at the post office on Mill Street. Though it would later be given in evidence that the two had been to Baltinglass a few weeks previously, presumably doing reconnaissance, they had to spend some time making sure there was no phone in the village. Once they were satisfied no one could telephone for help they took the attaché case from the cab and told Smith to wait outside the post office – they'd be back in ten minutes.

A curious aspect of the bank raid was that at no time did the two make any effort to conceal their identities. It was as though such precautions were somehow unnecessary. Perhaps they thought that in the chaos of the times they could get away with whatever they wanted, having no fear of any consequences.

Jordan and McMullen walked the short distance down Mill Street and over the wide stone bridge that crossed the River Slaney. At 2.10 p.m. they entered the National Bank on the main street. After Jordan asked for the manager the two took their guns from the attaché case and went behind the counter. When bank manager Maurice Wolfe opened his door Jordan levelled his revolver, shouting, 'Hands Up! Hand over your keys!'

McMullen and Jordan can hardly have anticipated the resistance they were going to face that day. If they had, they would surely have thought better of it because it was consistent and determined. Just why they should have encountered such opposition is not clear. But, again, it might be attributed to the atmosphere of the time when people had become used to violence. Baltinglass had seen its fair share of trouble during the War of Independence – a detachment of Black and Tans had been garrisoned in the village – and during the Civil War Baltinglass had twice been the scene of fighting. But, whatever the reason, over the next few minutes a number of people risked their lives to stop the thieves and Jordan and McMullen would leave the village empty-handed, having shot two men, one of whom was a mortally wounded policeman. Ultimately, the raid would also cost Felix McMullen his life.

The raiders' problems started almost immediately: the bank manager put his hand into his pocket and, instead of taking out the safe keys, as had been demanded, took out a .25 revolver and pointed it at Jordan. Afterwards Wolfe said that he wanted 'to shoot him dead and grapple with the other' but, at the telling moment, he had not been able to bring himself to shoot someone in cold blood. For a few seconds there was a standoff. Then McMullen produced his gun and shot Wolfe. As he fell to the floor Wolfe fired a shot to help raise the alarm. As he cried for help McMullen told him to shut up or he'd 'blow his brains out'.

The raiders then turned their attention to a young bank official, Cecil Shade, ordering him to open the safe. But, instead of instantly obeying the orders of the armed men, Shade tried to throw a set of keys out the window. After repeated threats he was stopped.

Meanwhile, another bank official had been hiding money from the cash drawers in a cupboard. Though he too stopped when threatened the raiders were far from being in control of the situation.

Then, to make matters worse, Mrs Wolfe came into the banking hall from upstairs. When she saw that her husband had been shot she ran out into the street calling for help. McMullen went after her, threatening to shoot her if she didn't stop but she kept running. McMullen then went back inside the bank and bolted the front door shut.

Meanwhile, Jordan had found a set of keys. Giving them to Shade he ordered him to open the safe. To buy time Shade fumbled with each key. None of them fitted the lock. But Shade already knew that because, in the confusion, he had managed to throw the safe keys out the window.

Then came the shrill call of a police whistle.

Outside was twenty-seven-year-old Sergeant Patrick O'Halloran. Originally from Gort, County Galway, he had been stationed in Baltinglass since the Civic Guards had been set up eighteen months before. While Sergeant O'Halloran was kicking in the door he was joined by Joseph Germaine, a civilian. Germaine had brought a gun. It was a Colt automatic, fully loaded.

Realising the raid was over Jordan and McMullen ran out of the back door. As they came out of the laneway at the side of the bank they ignored the sergeant's calls to stop. Germaine gave his gun to the sergeant and the guard started running after the raiders. By the time McMullen and Jordan were crossing back over the bridge the sergeant was just a few yards behind. He called on them to stop and pointed Germaine's gun at them. Then there was a puff of smoke and the sound of a shot. Later in court, contradictory evidence would be given relating to this part of the incident. Some witnesses said McMullen turned and, while moving in a backwards direction, facing the guard, fired the shot. McMullen said he had just pointed the gun behind him and fired blindly as he ran. But, whatever happened, Sergeant O'Halloran fell wounded with the safety catch of his Colt revolver still on.

When the two got back to the taxi there was no sign of the driver but, as Jordan tried to jump-start the car, Smith came out of a pub. McMullen shouted at him to get in the car and drive as fast as he could. Smith did as he was told – he saw that one of the men was armed.

When they reached the outskirts of Dublin, they stopped for a drink at the Templeogue Inn – at the raiders' invitation the taxi driver joined them. Once their thirsts were slaked they continued their journey. Near Terenure Jordan and McMullen got out and refused to pay the £5 fare.

Smith went straight to the police to report what happened. When he got to the station word of the Baltinglass raid had just arrived and guards had been dispatched minutes before to watch the road from that direction. McMullen and Jordan had only just eluded capture.

Meanwhile, back in Baltinglass, Sergeant O'Halloran lay badly wounded on the bridge. The bullet fired by McMullen had caused severe internal injuries. He was brought to the Curragh Military Hospital for emergency treatment but died of his wounds at 3.00 p.m. the following day.

The killing of Sergeant O'Halloran caused considerable shock in the country. He was only the third member of the new unarmed police force to have been killed in the line of duty. His death raised the fundamental question as to whether or not the new Civic Guards should be an armed force or not. At O'Halloran's funeral Eoin O'Duffy, Commissioner of the Civic Guards, said that 'a martyr's blood flowed on the streets of Baltinglass'. On the question of arming the police he said that, 'If it is the wish of the people that the guards be armed that wish will be carried out. It is the people who must decide to place arms in our hands.' However, in the debate there was little reference to the distinct possibility that

O'Halloran may not have been shot had he not been carrying the gun given to him by Germaine.

Hunt for the Killers

Colonel David Neligan was put in charge of the investigation. Neligan had once worked for the British administration but during the War of Independence he had changed sides and provided information to the republicans – he became known as Michael Collins' 'spy in the Castle'. After independence he became Director of Intelligence in the new Free State Army and was in charge of the detective branch of the guards. Neligan ordered an extensive manhunt for the killers of Sergeant O'Halloran.

When a number of early arrests yielded nothing Neligan put an undercover guard on the case. It was then that he learned of McMullen and Jordan's involvement.

On 14 February, Neligan called to Jordan's mother. He told her he was an old army comrade of her son's and had important news for him. Did she know where he was? She told him he had gone to Monaghan town the previous night. Fearing that Jordan might skip across the border Neligan immediately sent four members of the guards' elite Flying Squad by car to Monaghan. Peter Jordan was arrested shortly after 6 o'clock the next morning.

When Jordan was brought to Dublin and was picked out in an identity parade by the taxi driver who had brought them to Baltinglass, he admitted taking part in the raid, but said that at no stage did he shoot at anyone. It was McMullen who had fired the shots.

Acting on information given by Jordan, the guards searched his room and found the bank manager's revolver hidden. When they searched an avenue leading to Airlawn House, Terenure, they found two .45 Webley and one .45 Smith & Wesson revolvers, two trench coats and two grey caps that had been dumped by Jordan and McMullen after the raid.

Detectives then raided Felix McMullen's brother's house in

Athlone. McMullen wasn't there but they found a letter from him that, foolishly, had a return address in Liverpool. When the Liverpool police were contacted they raided the house, took Felix McMullen into custody and returned him to Dublin.

When the police showed McMullen a copy of Jordan's statement he said nothing at first. But when the revolvers, coats and caps found in Terenure were shown to him he obviously decided the game was up. He identified his trench coat and Webley and then said he'd 'tell them the whole thing'.

From the very start Jordan and McMullen had each tried to lay the greater part of the blame on the other. While Jordan made it clear that he had not fired a shot – and therefore, in his eyes, was not responsible for the death of the guard – McMullen tried to show that Jordan had been the leader: the robbery was Jordan's idea; Jordan rang for the taxi; Jordan told the taxi driver where to go; and Jordan had gone into the bank first.

McMullen admitted to shooting at both the bank manager and the guard but he said that both were accidents. He claimed he shot the bank manager when some of the bank staff knocked against him, causing him to pull the trigger. When the guard chased him across the bridge he had just put the gun behind his back and fired, to ward him off. He had no intention of shooting him, let alone killing him and it was only when he read the next day's newspapers that he knew the sergeant had been hit.

On Tuesday 18 February 1924 Felix McMullen and Peter Jordan were charged with armed robbery, wounding Maurice Wolfe and murdering Sergeant O'Halloran.

The First Trial

McMullen and Jordan's trial opened on Monday 7 July 1924 and lasted two days. It was presided over by seventy-three-year-old Judge O'Shaughnessy.

The essential facts of the case were agreed by each side – the two defendants had given statements admitting their involvement in the raid – and their lack of disguise meant they had been identified by a large number of witnesses. The two main points of contention at the trial were which of the two had been the leader and whether or not Felix McMullen had intended to shoot Sergeant O'Halloran.

McMullen's defence counsel said that it had not been McMullen's intention to shoot the guard – there was a great difference between robbing a bank and deliberately committing murder. They asked the jury to take into consideration McMullen's good, honest and upright character – Colonel Patrick Dalton, McMullen's commanding officer in the army, said he was a first class officer who had been both sober and trustworthy.

The prosecution argued that the crime was a capital crime. If a man were attempting to commit a felony and killed someone in the process, that crime would be murder and nothing else. The killing of O'Halloran was 'murder, unmistakable and without qualifying essence'. Because they were acting in concert in the crime both Jordan and McMullen were equally guilty of wilful and deliberate murder.

In his summing-up Judge O'Shaughnessy said that the two men had been conclusively identified as the men who had taken part in the bank raid. They were carrying out a felonious intent and, if one of them caused the death of the guard, then they were both equally guilty of murder, as each was abetting the other. The judge's direction could not have been clearer. There was ample and convincing evidence to find both guilty of murder. However, the jury had different ideas.

For two-and-a-half hours what can only be described as a series of confrontations took place between O'Shaughnessy and the foreman of the jury. The foreman said that the jury was unable to agree a verdict on the murder charge and asked if they could return a verdict of manslaughter. The judge told them they could return only a verdict of guilty, or not guilty, of murder. However, the jury continued to refuse to come to agreement on the murder charge. The judge was incredulous that they were failing to take his direction on a legal matter – a jury was not allowed to change the charge at a trial. When the judge commented that he 'deeply regretted' that a jury should behave in such a manner, the foreman replied, clearly nonplussed, 'Your lordship can draw your own inference.' The attitude of the jury might again have been ascribed to the peculiar atmosphere of the time when the most basic of issues – who had the right to determine law – was open to being questioned.

Faced with the jury's intransigence, the judge reluctantly ordered a retrial, which was fixed for Thursday 10 July.

Retrial

At the second trial the same evidence was produced as in the first. At the end, similar arguments to the ones made at the first were presented.

On this occasion the jury had little difficulty in reaching a decision. In fact, they took just forty minutes to return a verdict of not guilty of murder for Peter Jordan and a guilty verdict for Felix McMullen, with 'a strong recommendation to mercy'. The jury had obviously made a distinction between McMullen, who had fired the shot that killed the guard, and Jordan, who had not.

Judge O'Shaughnessy then put on his black cap and sentenced McMullen to death. McMullen told the court, 'I am very sorry that the guard was killed, but I never fired a shot with the intention of killing anyone.' His execution date was fixed for 1 August 1924.

Appeal

McMullen's defence counsel appealed against his conviction. It was the first appeal to be lodged in the Free State subsequent to the

1924 Courts of Justice Act. As the legal apparatus contained in the act had yet to be set up fully – even the envelopes used to send legal documents had 'On His Majesty's Service' crossed out and 'Saorstat Eireann' written in hand – his hearing had to wait until a Court of Criminal Appeal could be formally established.

The new Court of Appeal heard its first case on 21 and 22 July. McMullen's appeal was made on three grounds: that the jury in the first trial had the right to find a verdict of manslaughter; that the judge did not have the right to refuse the jury finding another verdict than murder; that in point of fact the jury had agreed, they agreed to find the defendant guilty of manslaughter and such a verdict should have been recorded – therefore, the second trial was a nullity.

The Court of Appeal dismissed the arguments. It said that the judge had clearly directed the jury that there was 'not a shred of evidence of manslaughter' and that the killing of a police officer in the course of a felony was murder 'from the earliest times'. The killing of the guard was murder, regardless of whether McMullen actually intended to hit him or not because McMullen obviously did not have the gun that day for show and had already shot the bank manager and threatened to 'blow his brains out'. The evidence of witnesses, who had said that McMullen had turned around on the bridge, took aim and fired at the guard, was reiterated.

When the Executive Council of the Free State, headed by Liam Cosgrave, with Kevin O'Higgins as Minister for Justice, met on 28 July it decided that 'the case was not one calling for a recommendation for mercy'. From their standpoint the refusal was quite reasonable – after all, a member of the guards, carrying out his duty, had been gunned down in broad daylight. It also sent out a message that such reckless acts of lawlessness leading to loss of life, especially the life of a policeman on duty, would not be tolerated.

There were several petitions sent to the government pleading for clemency from jurors from the first trial who had disagreed with the murder charge, from jurors from the second trial who had also favoured a manslaughter charge and from the manager and staff of the Baltinglass bank. But they amounted to nothing: Felix McMullen was executed in Mountjoy Prison at 8.00 a.m. on Friday 1 August 1924.

In the meantime, Peter Jordan remained in prison, having been sentenced to twenty lashes and ten years' penal servitude. However, he did not serve his full sentence. In 1926, when the country had settled from the upheaval of the Civil War, he was released from prison.

7 Cornelius O'Leary, Cork

Executed on 28 July 1925 for the murder of Patrick O'Leary

Patrick O'Leary's Wake

On 8 March 1924 the bizarre wake of forty-six-year-old Patrick O'Leary took place at the O'Leary family's three-roomed cottage in Kilkerran, not far from the village of Clonakilty in west Cork.

The O'Learys were a longstanding family in the area. They lived in a small cottage on a 40-acre farm with good land, half a dozen cows and two horses. There had originally been eight children in the O'Leary family. One had died some years before and of the remaining siblings, three had moved away which left the oldest son Patrick, his brother Con and sisters Hannah and Maryanne in Kilkerran. All were single and, except for Maryanne, lived with their elderly mother. The father of the house, Patrick Sr, was dead and according to the terms of the will his wife inherited the farm. On her death it would pass to the next in line, Patrick.

Patrick was the eldest son and was described as a large, stout man who weighed somewhere between 11 and 12 stone. He smoked a pipe and had a thin, dark moustache. Patrick worked the farm and acted like the boss of the house. He was loud, talkative, bossy and, some said, 'kind of quarrelsome'. In a somewhat unusual arrangement he slept in a loft in the barn. This was believed to have been out of choice – the alternative would have been to share a bed with Con in the house and it was known the two did not get on.

Con was about forty years old and weighed 11 stone. He was a much different character to Patrick. He was a quiet, almost introverted, man. He was also described as 'restless'.

All that is known about Hannah is that she was the quietest of them all.

In contrast to the others, Maryanne was described as a pleasant, good-tempered woman. Perhaps it was for this reason that she did not live in the family home, but with an elderly female neighbour.

At the wake Patrick's siblings and mother were joined by neighbours and friends. However, what made this wake unusual was that the open coffin on the table contained only parts of the dead man's remains. The reason for this was that Patrick O'Leary had been murdered, decapitated and his body hacked into bits in circumstances that were gruesome in the extreme. Patrick's family were the main suspects so, along with those paying their respects, a number of on-duty Civic Guards were also present.

The first part of Patrick to be discovered was found on the afternoon of 7 March, the day before the wake, by a ten-year-old boy who had been tending cows in a nearby field. Noticing a bloodstained potato sack under some furze bushes he opened it and came face to face with a badly beaten and decomposing head. It was later ascertained that it had been struck a number of times on the right-hand side. Such had been the violence of the blows that the side of the skull had been reduced to pulp.

The guards were called and soon after they arrived Patrick's right arm, severed at the shoulder, was found. Later that evening, his gutted torso was added to the macabre collection.

The guards recognised the man but they wanted a formal

identification by a family member. Given the circumstances of the finds they also wanted to see the reactions to the discoveries.

By the time Con O'Leary was brought to the field it was dark. When they took the head out of the sack the guards shone torches to help him see. Con looked at the head for some time before saying, 'Yes, that is my brother Pat.'

'Con, are you sure now?' the sergeant asked.

'Yes, that's my brother Pat all right.'

At that point a garda inspector arrived. However, when he asked Con if he could identify the head he said he couldn't. When the sergeant asked, 'How is it you identified it for me and you cannot identify it now?' Con said nothing.

Patrick's head, arm and torso were then brought to the back room of a pub in the nearby village of Milltown. Lit by candles and a bicycle lamp, the head was rested on a bit of hay on a table.

When Patrick's sister Hannah was brought in, she looked at the head for a while, but did not take any particular interest in it – she looked at it, then looked around the room. When asked about the distinctive bald temples on each side of the head she looked briefly and turned away. She said she did not know who it was.

Hannah was then brought out of the room and her sister Maryanne was brought in. Unlike Con and Hannah, Maryanne had no problem identifying her brother.

When Hannah was brought back in, Maryanne identified Patrick in front of her. Then Hannah agreed it was their brother.

The two sisters were taken out and Con was brought in. When he looked at the head he said he could not be sure, but that he thought it was 'like Paddy's poll'. Then Con started rubbing his hands together saying, 'I am innocent. I am innocent, my hands are clean.'

The guards considered the behaviour of Con and Hannah as being particularly suspicious.

When the guards searched the barn where Patrick slept it was discovered that the rafters immediately above the bed were stained with blood. Other boards appeared to have been recently washed but when examined more closely blood was found in woodworm holes. There were also bloodstains under the bed.

It was obvious to the police that someone had gone into Patrick's loft and struck him violently on the head. Death was caused by a fracture of the skull. The wounds were circular in shape and the guards believed the injuries could have been inflicted with a stone. It was not known whether Patrick had been asleep at the time of the attack, but he had been lying on his left-hand side and there were no signs of a struggle.

Whoever killed Patrick had taken his body and dissected it in the most gruesome manner. The cuts were jagged and it was suggested that a reaping hook found in the loft, or possibly a blunt carving knife, had been used to hack up the body.

At the wake, the local sergeant overheard a conversation between a neighbouring farmer, William Whelton, and Con in which Whelton said, 'I must certainly say, Con, it is a terrible state of affairs to see your brother cut up there in pieces and you not a bit worried over it. I must also say, Con, that suspicions are strongly against you and it is up to you to find the perpetrator and free yourself.' Con, standing beside the fireplace in the kitchen, rubbed his hands together again and said, 'I am innocent, any way my hands are clean.'

Another neighbour, Mrs McCarthy, said loudly to Mrs O'Leary, 'It's a shame, Mrs O'Leary, to see your son in such a state – it is easily known who done it.' Although the comment was not addressed at Con he said, 'I am innocent.'

At the end of this strange evening Con, Hannah and Mrs O'Leary went to bed at around 12 o'clock. Maryanne was the only member of the O'Leary family to stay in the room with the coffin and the only company she had was that of a policeman.

Discovery of More Body Parts

In the days following the wake the guards continued their search for Patrick's remains. Interestingly, none of the family offered to help in the search.

In the end, eight parts of Patrick's body were found – all were found within 650 yards of the O'Leary cottage. Patrick's right leg was in a gorse-covered field, his left in the ruins of an old house and his left arm in a marshy field. Patrick's coat and trousers were found when a guard noticed that he was being watched by Hannah and Mrs O'Leary while searching a certain area – their interest had led him to believe that he was near an area where he would make another find. One of the last discoveries was perhaps the most gruesome. A guard searching near the O'Leary house saw the family's sheepdog emerge from some furze with something in its mouth. When he caught the dog the 'something' turned out to be Patrick's right arm that had had almost all the flesh eaten off it.

On 14 March Mrs O'Leary, Con, Hannah and Maryanne were all arrested and charged with the murder of Patrick on 26 February 1925. Con said nothing when charged, Hannah said, 'I had nothing to do with it', Mrs O'Leary made no statement and Maryanne said she had not been in the family house at all that night.

Trials, Execution and Prison

While all four remaining members of the O'Leary family who had been living in Kilkerran when Patrick was killed were charged, only Con and Hannah were returned for trial. While awaiting her trial Maryanne O'Leary died in Mountjoy Prison – it was reported that a bad eye condition had become cancerous. Although she could never clear her name in court, it was likely that Maryanne had nothing to do with the crime and had indeed been out of the house the night Patrick was killed. Owing to Mrs O'Leary's old age and frail condition her trial was initially deferred and later dropped.

On 23 June 1925 the trial of Con and Hannah O'Leary began. They were charged with murder and conspiracy to murder. Both pleaded not guilty. After two days of evidence the jury failed to reach a verdict and a retrial was ordered.

The second trial opened the following week and again lasted two days.

According to the prosecution, 'nothing the jury ever read could surpass the horrible brutality associated with the murder. It was almost inconceivable that beast, not men or women, could behave to the remains of the murdered man as this wretched man's body was treated by those in immediate contact with him.'

Neither Con nor Hannah gave evidence. Con followed the trial with interest but Hannah was nearly always hidden from view by her shawl.

A central issue at the trial had been the relationships between members of the O'Leary family, in particular that between Patrick and Con.

The two brothers were known not to get on. In fact, the two had not spoken to each other for the previous four or five years – even before their father's death. During the course of a day the brothers' paths rarely crossed – Patrick got up early and at the end of the day Con only went into the house after Patrick had gone to the barn.

A major cause of bad feeling between the brothers was that Con, though he lived in the house, did not work on the family farm. He worked for another farmer called Travers, which left Patrick to do the work of two men. In the past, Patrick had told Travers that he did not want Con working for him. Patrick believed that Con should either work on the family farm or get out of the area altogether.

Towards the end of February, the week of the murder, tensions within the family appear to have been high. The immediate reason seems to have been Patrick's refusal to hand over money he made at a fair to their mother. Mrs O'Leary and Maryanne had asked the parish priest to intervene in the dispute but, for some unknown reason, changed their minds and withdrew the request for help. A short time later Patrick was killed, chopped up and his body scattered in the fields around Kilkerran.

On the night of Monday 25 February Hannah and Maryanne saw Patrick go to the barn sometime between 9 and 10 o'clock. According to Hannah and Mrs O'Leary, Patrick came into the house early the next morning and then went to the Bandon fair to sell a colt. This was what Hannah and her mother told Maryanne, who had not stayed in the house that night, when she came into the house that morning.

When the family was questioned as to why they had not raised the alarm after Patrick had been missing for a number of days, and the horse he was supposed to have been going to sell was still in the field, they said they assumed he had just gone off for a while for a 'lark'. They expected Patrick to return at any time. Con had said, 'Wisha, I didn't think it necessary.'

Con's employer Travers said that three days after the last sighting of Patrick, when he went with Con to the Rosscarbery Fair, Con had insisted on travelling by a route that would not take them past the O'Leary cottage. The prosecution's implication was that there was something happening at the O'Leary house that Con did not want Travers to see.

Two new pieces of evidence were produced at the trial. One was that on the morning of 7 March – the day the first parts of Patrick body were discovered – Con had gone to the family solicitor to inspect the terms of their father's will. Did Con go to check that he was next in line to inherit the farm? The other was that a piece of bloodstained quilt and bed ticking found under Hannah and Mrs O'Leary's bed matched ones that had been found in the loft where Patrick slept. For reasons the guards did not explain, these had only been found on 20 March, days after the family home had been first searched.

At the trial it was never outlined who had struck the fatal blows that killed Patrick, who dissected the body, nor what collusion there must have been in order to carry out and cover up the killing.

There was virtually no direct or circumstantial evidence against Hannah except for her hesitation in identifying her brother and that she was in the house the night it was believed Patrick was killed. In his summing-up, Judge Hanna outlined his own thoughts of what Hannah's role might have been. He said that changing bloodstained bed clothes for clean ones 'might be a woman's job'. He also said 'I think it would go far beyond the annals of crime in the history of this country to think that any woman could carve through the flesh of a man's thighs with a chopper or hatchet and nick the bone and break it in two. It may occur to you that that was a man's job.'

After an absence of fifty-two minutes the jury found both Con and Hannah O'Leary guilty of the murder of their brother, with a recommendation of mercy for Hannah.

When they were sentenced, Hannah replied, 'I did not kill my brother' and Con said, 'I had not hand, act, or part in the murder. I am going to die an innocent man.'

On the eve of her execution date Hannah O'Leary was reprieved by the Governor General and ordered to serve penal servitude for life.

Con went to his death on the morning of 28 July 1925 and was buried in the grounds of the prison.

Mrs O'Leary, whose trial never went ahead, was released from prison. She returned to west Cork and the family home in Kilkerran, where she died in January 1928.

Hannah, confined in Mountjoy Women's Prison (now St Patrick's), became the last surviving member of the O'Leary family who had once lived together in Kilkerran. As time went on the prison authorities were willing to release her. However, according to the official papers, Hannah O'Leary was 'not quite normal' and therefore they would not release her unless there was someone who would look after her. As she had no family left, she remained in prison for longer than nearly any other woman in twentieth-century Ireland. In 1942, after serving over seventeen years, fifty-six-year-old Hannah was finally released. However, this was only into the care of the Good Shepherd nuns who ran a Magdalen laundry.

8 and 9 Michael Talbot and Annie Walsh, Limerick

Executed on 5 August 1925 for the murder of Edward Walsh

Annie Walsh, Edward Walsh and Michael Talbot

On 5 August 1925 Annie Walsh of Fedamore, County Limerick, became the first woman to be executed in Ireland for over twenty years when she, along with her husband's nephew, Michael Talbot, was hanged for the murder of her husband, Edward Walsh. While Annie Walsh was the first woman to be executed after independence, she also holds the dubious distinction of being the only one to have been executed in the history of the state.

The story of how thirty-one-year-old Annie Walsh, née Barret and originally from Limerick City, and twenty-three-year-old Michael Talbot, a 'servant boy' who lived in Carnane, were to meet their fates in Mountjoy's execution chamber started shortly after 8.00 a.m. on 25 October 1924 when Annie banged on the door of Fedamore Civic Guard barracks. The guard who answered found her in an 'excited condition'.

'Tell the sergeant to come down immediately,' she said, clapping her hands together. 'My husband was shot dead last night by Michael Talbot.'

When the sergeant came down she told him that the previous night she and her husband had been in bed when her husband's nephew Michael knocked on the front door around 10.30 p.m. Annie called out that it was 'after hours' and told him to go away. But the knocking became more and more insistent. Eventually, Michael broke the door open and told the couple to get out of bed. Annie and Edward went into the kitchen and the three sat in front of the fire. Apparently the men had a friendly conversation but, around midnight, the mood changed when Michael told Annie to put out the lamp. When she refused there was an argument and Michael hit her (the guards noted a small bruise under her left eye). Michael then stood up and punched Edward, after which he took out a revolver and shot his uncle in the head.

When the sergeant asked why she had not come earlier, she said that Michael had held her down by the throat for the whole night. From what the guards knew of past relations between Annie and Michael, all of this would have made sense. Michael had only recently been released from Limerick Prison after serving four months for assaulting Annie.

A guard rushed on ahead by bicycle and when he got to the Walshs' cottage he found Edward lying dead in a pool of blood on the kitchen floor – the room was in a state of disorder, as if there had been a struggle. The dead man was fully dressed, even down to cap and unlaced boots.

When a local doctor, Dr Hedderman, called he examined the body but was not able to find any evidence of a bullet wound. When he searched the room he did not find a bullet or evidence of a ricochet. The guards also established that, though the neighbouring houses were less than 25 yards away, no one had heard a gunshot during the night.

The doctor discovered that Edward had not been shot but had suffered a depressed fracture of his skull about an inch in diameter and another wound about two inches long that had cracked his skull. Both, Dr Hedderman concluded, had been caused by the blow of a heavy blunt instrument and either could have caused his death.

It did not take long for the guards to apprehend Michael Talbot. He was found before midday hiding in a loft in his mother's house. When he was arrested what might have appeared a straightforward investigation became considerably more complex when he told the guards, 'You may arrest Mrs Walsh as well as me.'

Michael then gave a version of events quite different to that given by Annie.

'I did not kill him,' he said. 'She killed him. I held his hands while she killed him. She struck him two blows and he died.' Michael said that when he called to the house he was let in. After about two hours Annie asked Edward to go outside to get a stick for the fire. While he was out she picked up a hatchet and concealed it under her apron. When Edward returned and sat down she struck him on the head, knocking him to the floor. 'I held his hands,' Michael repeated, 'while she struck him another blow on the head.'

Michael said that the reason she had killed her husband was to get compensation for his death. Michael made reference to compensation that Annie had received after his previous assault on her – 'Wasn't she able to get £20 over the last case?' He said that when she got compensation for her husband, 'She was to divide it with me … I was to keep out of the way until she got the money.' Then Michael hinted that the two had been having some sort of relationship. 'She was to come to me and we were to go away together. I will show ye the hatchet she killed him with. I stayed in the house all night with her until 6.30 a.m. She said she was going to tell [Edward's sister] Alice and the guards that Ned is dead.'

After hearing this version of events the guards brought Michael to the Walsh house where Edward's wake had started. When they found two hatchets Michael pointed to the larger one and said that was the one Annie had used to kill her husband.

When Annie was arrested on suspicion of killing Edward she protested. 'I did not kill my husband,' she said. 'I swear to that.'

'You killed him with the hatchet,' Michael said.

'You are a liar,' Annie snapped back. 'You killed him.'

By the time they were brought to William Street Barracks in Limerick the next day neither had given a statement. That evening the guards brought Annie and Michael together for their tea, to see what would happen. They were not disappointed with the results.

The very sight of Annie prompted Michael to give a statement. He told the guards more or less what he had said when arrested. But he added one more bit of information, 'On Thursday night, 23 October 1924, I met Annie Walsh at the cross leading to her own house. She asked me to come to her house on Friday night, 24 October, to kill Edward Walsh, her husband.' While the guards were taking down all of this, Annie kept calling Michael a liar. When he was finished, Michael signed the statement.

Annie, now furious, said she wanted to give a statement. 'The statement made by Michael Talbot is lies,' she said. This time Michael continually interrupted her as she repeated what she had already told the guards, adding that Michael had been drunk.

When she signed her statement it was Michael's turn again; 'Annie Walsh's statement is wrong. The door was open when I came … I had no revolver. I was not drunk. I never had a revolver in my life. I stopped until morning with Mrs Walsh. I did not hold her down by the throat …'

Shortly afterwards, both Annie and Michael were charged with Edward Walsh's murder.

Trials

Though they were accused of taking part in the same crime the two were tried separately so that the evidence against each could be clearly presented. Michael's trial was on 9 July and Annie's the following day. As was the norm for many years, their junior counsels were up against far more capable and experienced senior counsels, leaving both defendants at a distinct disadvantage.

According to the judges at each of their trials it had not been necessary for the juries to decide whose hand had delivered the fatal blows. If they believed that the crime was carried out between them, then each was as guilty as the other. It didn't matter who had actually struck Edward.

Though the relationships between Edward and Annie Walsh, and that between Annie and Michael Talbot were central to the case there was scant information presented.

Annie and Edward had been married for seven years. Edward was described as a man in his sixties who was 'semi-independent financially' – he was a man who was a cut above the labouring class. Though they were not known to have had a difficult relationship the difference in ages between them might have been an issue. Though such an arrangement was far more common in the 1920s than it is today, there is some evidence that it was a factor. Edward was described as 'not very robust', while Annie had also been in the habit of entertaining young men, playing cards and singing songs in the house, late into the night. Edward called it 'blackguarding' and it was stopped after a police raid one night. Added to this slightly circumspect evidence a guard reported that after the killing Annie told him, 'I am rid of the Walshs now,' which hardly indicated an endearing relationship between the couple.

Despite the previous assault it was evident that Michael and Annie had had a reconciliation and, for at least some time prior to the killing, were having some sort of relationship. Michael's stated motive was that after Edward was killed and the compensation money paid he and Annie would run away together. He said they had slept together after Edward had been killed and among his possessions when arrested was Annie's wedding ring.